W9-CNO-242

THE GREENHOUSE EFFECT

KATHLYN GAY

THE GREEN-HOUSE EFFECT

FRANKLIN WATTS/A SCIENCE IMPACT BOOK
NEW YORK/LONDON/TORONTO/SYDNEY/1986 A GROLIER COMPANY

Library of Congress Cataloging in Publication Data
Gay, Kathlyn.
The greenhouse effect.
(A Science impact book)
Bibliography: p.
Includes index.
Summary: Examines evidence that rising levels
of carbon dioxide in the atmosphere may be
changing the earth's climate. Also discusses
how and why scientists study climatic changes.
1. Greenhouse effect, Atmospheric—Juvenile
literature.   2. Climatic changes—Juvenile literature.
[1. Greenhouse effect, Atmospheric.   2. Climatic
changes]   I. Title.   II. Series.
QC912.3.G39   1986   363.7'392   85-26486
ISBN 0-531-10154-1

CONTENTS

THE GREENHOUSE EFFECT

CHAPTER ONE

THE CARBON DIOXIDE QUESTION

Can We Delay A Greenhouse Warming? is the question posed in the title of a September 1983 report from the U.S. Environmental Protection Agency (EPA). Another study by the U.S. National Academy of Sciences (NAS), released a few days after the EPA report, is simply titled *Changing Climate.* Both publications deal with the same problem: what to do about the buildup of carbon dioxide in the atmosphere, a phenomenon that is raising the temperature of the earth and could change weather patterns worldwide.

Yet the two federal reports are quite different in tone and approach. The EPA document implies that drastic action is needed now to prevent a crisis brought on by climatic changes. The NAS study says its "stance is conservative" and urges "caution, not panic," in trying to develop solutions to the so-called greenhouse effect or carbon dioxide threat, as some have labeled it.

THE GREENHOUSE THEORY

The warming of the earth became a major concern in the United States after a 1965 report to the president on the quality of the environment warned that carbon dioxide concentrations in the air were increasing. Since that time numerous magazine and newspaper articles and major studies have addressed the issue. But the greenhouse effect has really been recognized for a much longer period.

More than a century ago, scientists developed theories about climatic changes that could be linked to minute changes in the composition of the atmosphere. A Swedish chemist, Svante Arrhenius, coined the greenhouse term in 1896, when he noted similarities between the earth's atmosphere and the glass enclosures of a greenhouse: both allow the sunlight to enter but prevent most of the solar heat from escaping.

While a glass or plastic greenhouse keeps plants warm by holding in heat and inhibiting air movement, the greenhouse effect on earth is a different matter. The earth's atmosphere is highly transparent to short-wavelength energy or sunlight. But when visible light reflects from the earth's surface, energy is converted to a long-wavelength infrared radiation. The radiation or heat is absorbed ("held") by partially opaque trace gases in the atmosphere, primarily water vapor and carbon dioxide. The latter measures about 340 parts per million (ppm)—or 340 molecules of carbon dioxide for every one million molecules of air. Other gases such as methane also "trap" infrared radiation. By absorbing heat, the gas molecules increase in temperature, and the heat then reradiates from the atmosphere in all directions, with some going back to the ground and some out into space.

The greenhouse effect is what makes the earth habitable. Without water vapor, carbon dioxide, and other trace gases, too much heat would escape and the earth would probably be too cold to sustain life. The situation would resemble that on Mars, where there is little carbon dioxide and no water vapor.

Yet an increase in the carbon dioxide content of the atmosphere may be creating too much of a "blanket" for the earth. Although there is no evidence that carbon dioxide is increasing so rapidly that it will suffocate or "melt" the earth, it is the buildup of greenhouse gases—the *enhanced* greenhouse effect usually referred to as simply "the greenhouse effect" —that has brought about so much scientific inquiry and uncertainty in recent years.

THE CARBON CYCLE

For about 600 million years, the atmosphere has consisted of 78 percent nitrogen and 21 percent oxygen. That leaves just 1 percent for other gases, including carbon dioxide, which makes up only .03 percent of the atmosphere's dry weight.

This trace of carbon dioxide is essential for life. Green plants absorb carbon dioxide from the air. In a process known as *photosynthesis* (from two Greek words meaning "putting together with light"), the green pigment chlorophyll in plants captures sunlight and uses solar energy to combine carbon dioxide and water, producing glucose—a carbohydrate foodstuff that is an important source of energy for animals and people. During the process plants give off oxygen as a waste product, which is inhaled by animals and people, who in turn exhale carbon dioxide produced when food is oxidized, or "burned"—used by their bodies.

Because of this continual process, the supply of carbon dioxide and oxygen remains fairly stable on earth. So why is carbon dioxide increasing in the atmosphere? Where does it come from?

Carbon—one of the most important chemical elements—usually combines with other elements to form compounds (such as carbon dioxide, a compound of carbon and oxygen). All living things are made up of carbon compounds, which seem unlimited in their

THE GREENHOUSE EFFECT

CARBON DIOXIDE

1. Burning of fossil fuels and elimination of trees increase carbon dioxide (CO_2) in the atmosphere.

2. The earth's surface radiates heat. Some escapes, but the CO_2 traps the rest, increasing the temperature.

3. The warming increases water vapor in the air, which in turn absorbs more of the earth's heat.

4. Rising surface temperatures melt snow and ice. A poor reflector, the exposed ground absorbs more sunlight, and in turn melts more snow.

5. Oceans store more heat, extending the warming trend. Melting glacial ice causes oceans to swell.

variety. Thus living plants and animals are one source of carbon and the compound carbon dioxide. Other natural pools, or reservoirs, include the oceans and the atmosphere and fossilized forms of carbon such as oil, gas, and coal—deposited over millions of years. When the fossil fuels are burned, carbon dioxide is released.

"Carbon circulates naturally among these reservoirs driven by physical and biological forces; we term this circulation the carbon cycle . . ." say the National Research Council (NRC) scientists who prepared the 1983 assessment of the effects of carbon dioxide for the National Academy of Sciences (NAS). The report goes on to explain that carbon dioxide is also injected into the atmosphere by human activities, such as burning fossil fuels. Cutting down vast numbers of trees in tropical rain forests may also release substantial amounts of carbon dioxide that are not absorbed by photosynthesis. In effect, human activities increase the flow of carbon, redistributing it from one holding place to another.

Before there were widespread human activities on earth, "one part of the carbon cycle involved production of organic matter from atmospheric carbon dioxide and water and transporting of this material to the ocean where it was buried in marine sediments," says the NRC report, adding that this part of the cycle has been reversed due to personal and industrial use of fuels. "Some of the carbon stored over 500 million years in marine sediments is now returning to the atmosphere in a few short generations." And therein lies part of the problem—one reason for the increase of carbon dioxide in the atmosphere.

CARBON DIOXIDE BUILD-UP
Over eons the carbon dioxide level of the earth's atmosphere has fluctuated, but there has been just the right

amount of carbon dioxide and other trace gases to maintain a delicate balance between the solar energy reaching earth and the heat radiating out. In effect, carbon dioxide helps the atmosphere serve as a thermal blanket that warms the earth.

In just a little more than a century, however, carbon dioxide has been accumulating in the atmosphere at a steady (some observers say alarming) rate. The balance between the incoming and outgoing solar energy has to be established at a higher temperature. Thus, as the carbon dioxide increases, the average temperature of the earth rises also.

Although the levels of carbon dioxide and other trace gases have not increased in large amounts, the accumulation is nonetheless significant. Since about 1860, with the onset of the Industrial Revolution, scientists estimate that carbon dioxide concentrations have risen from 270–90 ppm to about 340 ppm today. However, accurate measurements of carbon dioxide buildup did not begin until 1957, when the Scripps Institute of Oceanography set up a monitoring laboratory atop Mauna Loa, a volcanic mountain in Hawaii. Far from sources of industrial pollution, the Pacific site is "ideal for monitoring large-scale changes in the atmosphere," writes John Gribbin, scientist and author of *Future Weather and the Greenhouse Effect.*

Mauna Loa measurements are often used in graph form (opposite) to illustrate reports and articles on the greenhouse effect—for good reason. As Dr. Gribbin explains it: "The Mauna Loa records show a seasonal fluctuation in carbon dioxide, ranging up and down 5 ppm . . . the effect of plants taking in carbon dioxide during Northern Hemisphere spring and summer, and releasing it as they drop their leaves and decay in the fall and winter." If a line were drawn to connect the uppermost points—the peaks—on the graph (see page 8), the buildup of carbon dioxide over three decades would become dramatically clear.

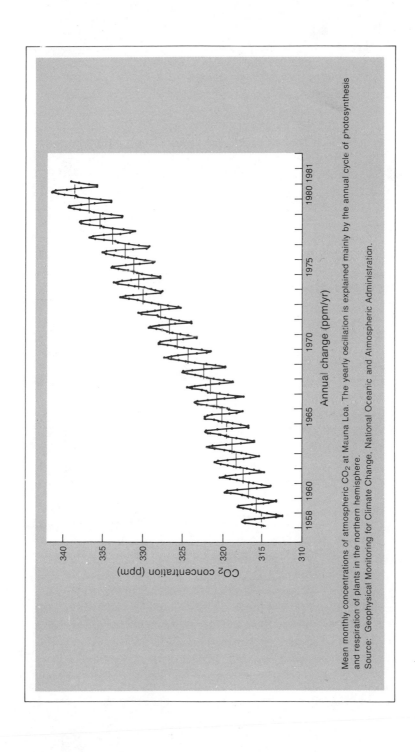

Mean monthly concentrations of atmospheric CO_2 at Mauna Loa. The yearly oscillation is explained mainly by the annual cycle of photosynthesis and respiration of plants in the northern hemisphere.

Source: Geophysical Monitoring for Climate Change, National Oceanic and Atmospheric Administration.

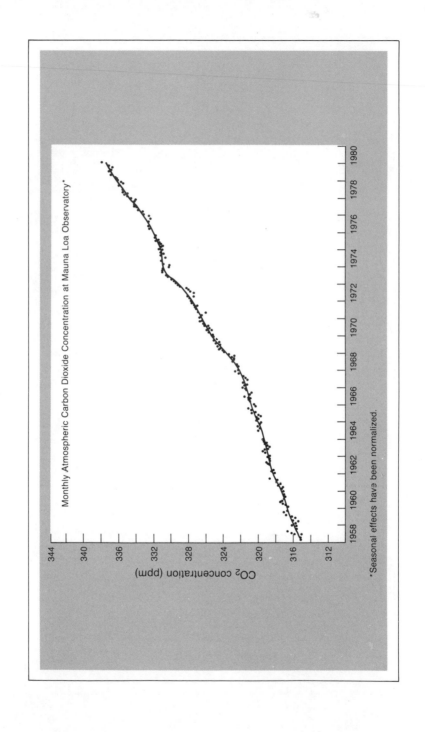

Monthly Atmospheric Carbon Dioxide Concentration at Mauna Loa Observatory*

CO_2 concentration (ppm)

*Seasonal effects have been normalized.

If the present rate of increase continues, the carbon dioxide concentration in the atmosphere could reach 500–600 ppm by the year 2040—double the level at the turn of this century. Scientists have not determined narrow temperature ranges on different parts of the earth, but they have estimated an equilibrium temperature increase as high as 3.6° F (2° C) by 2050–60 and 9° F (5° C) by 2100. Again the overall increase seems small, but not when viewed in terms of climatic changes over the past 125,000 years, during which temperatures have risen no more than 9° F. That increase could be equaled in just 120 years if the projected warming of the globe does occur!

In spite of such projections, many scientists share the view that if carbon dioxide buildup can be slowed down or maintained at the present level, concentrations would increase to no more than 420 ppm by the middle of the next century. But that depends on many factors—as does the very complex process of climatic change.

CHAPTER TWO

GATHERING CLIMATE DATA

If you don't like the weather, just stick around a few minutes—it will change!" That's common advice for people visiting Chicago, in the heart of the Midwest. During the spring and summer months especially, the weather in the Windy City can change rapidly. With an oncoming July rainstorm, for example, a bright sunny sky can suddenly cloud over and become as dark as night, and the temperature may plunge from a high of 95–100° F (about 35–38° C) to 55–60° F (about 13–15° C) in half an hour.

WEATHER VS. CLIMATE

Certainly other parts of the nation, continent, and world also experience dramatic short-term changes in the weather along with regular seasonal variations. But scientists distinguish between changing weather and climatic changes. Usually "weather" refers to the atmospheric state at a specific time and place. "Gusty winds," "low-lying fog," "high humidity," and "chance of showers" are a few terms weather forecasters use to describe the weather occurring over a few hours or days.

"Climate," although it deals with the same properties, describes weather conditions—including seasonal changes and temperature averages—over months, decades, centuries, or ages. Thus a climatic pattern is determined by weather statistics and is defined according to the average weather over a long-term period.

EVIDENCE OF PAST CLIMATES

In order to understand how climate changes and how it can be affected or modified by human activities, scientists study global weather over eons—billions of years. During past geologic eras, or time in millions of years (MA) on the geologic scale, temperatures have changed drastically in various parts of the earth, and the globe overall has alternately warmed and cooled.

Since the planet formed an estimated 4.5 to 5 billion years ago, a number of ice ages lasting thousands of years have occurred. Continents that are warm today were once covered by glaciers, or vast sheets of ice. Between the ice ages, there have been periods called interglacials, when global temperatures have risen and the ice has melted. The peak of the last ice age was about 25,000 years ago. For the past 10,000 years, a warming trend has prevailed and the earth has again been experiencing an interglacial period, although some scientists say we are on the verge of a new ice age.

How do scientists reach such conclusions? What types of data provide evidence of weather conditions millions of years before human civilization emerged? How do those data relate to climatic patterns today?

Evidence of ancient climates comes from studies in a variety of disciplines, particularly paleoclimatology (from the Greek word *paleo*, meaning "ancient," and *climatology*, the science of climate). Geology, physics, chemistry, oceanography, archeology, astronomy, meteorology, and more recently astrogeology (planet geology) and computer technology are other important fields that contribute to an understanding of climatic patterns.

Researchers in these fields use a variety of techniques to draw conclusions or to form theories about climate conditions eons ago. For example, studies of well-preserved sediments, fossilized forms of single-celled bacteria, and chemical deposits lead scientists to speculate that climatic conditions in the Precambrian Era—from about 4,600 MA (4.6 billion years ago) to 570 MA—were no doubt extreme in some parts of the globe, but in other areas temperatures were moderate enough (neither too cold nor too hot) for life to be established. Single-celled organisms were able to survive, and multicelled animals and plants evolved.

Climatic information for geologic ages prior to 570 MA is scanty, since much of the interpretation depends on geological evidence. The oldest discovered sedimentary rocks date from about 3,700 MA years ago. Such rocks tend to be so altered by heat and pressure that scientists have a difficult time gleaning climatic evidence from the formations. Scientists also lack detailed information about the position of the oceans and continents during the planet's first few billion years.

CONTINENTAL DRIFT

Geologists generally agree that a mass of evidence exists to link climatic changes with the concept of continental drift. According to this view, the continents were closely joined in a kind of "supercontinent" some 200 MA. The connecting land areas—sometimes called Pangea, meaning "all lands"—were surrounded by a huge sea. But over millions of years, the land areas, or continents, have been drifting apart, colliding, and breaking up again. Evidence of this drift became apparent when geographers centuries ago noted the shapes of the continents. If the land areas could be moved, they would fit together rather like parts of a jigsaw puzzle, as the maps opposite show.

Since the early nineteenth century, scientists have accumulated much physical evidence to support the idea of continental drift. For example, similar rock and fossil samples have been discovered on continents separated by oceans at latitudes different from where those samples could possibly have formed, suggesting that the continents were once aligned. Scientists also theorize that the Himalayas, the world's highest mountain ranges, were the result of continents colliding.

Climate has been affected by the breakup of landmasses because eons ago there was no land next to the poles. According to continental-drift theory, ocean currents brought waters from the equator to the poles, creating warmer conditions. But with the movement of landmasses over millions of years, warm water has not been able to circulate to the highest latitudes. Warm currents have also been blocked by continents grouping together around a polar sea. Ice covers, or caps, the water and reflects solar heat cooling the area even more, allowing an ice buildup on land.

TOOLS SCIENTISTS USE

Over this century—because of the many different tools and techniques developed to measure and analyze past climatic conditions—data related to climate have become more and more reliable. One important and now traditional tool is geologic dating, which has been accomplished by a variety of methods, including the measurement of radioactivity in the earth's sub-

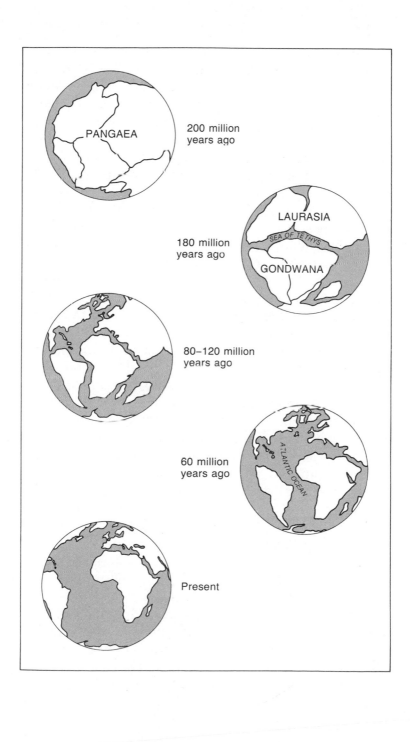

stances. Stephen H. Schneider, one of the world's leading climatologists, explains in *The Coevolution of Climate and Life* that radioactive atoms are believed to disintegrate at a constant rate "unchanged by chemical or physical alterations of the compounds in which the atoms are contained (such as rock, water, or air). The decay rate is expressed in terms of its half-life— that is, the time it takes for half the atoms originally present to decay into daughter products. . . . This rate of . . . decay is unaffected by temperature or pressure." Thus scientists can determine when the mineral or original element was formed, and then project the age of rocks and various earth strata.

"Radiocarbon dating" is probably a familiar term, and it is another important method used to reconstruct past climates. The amount of carbon-14 left in the remains of plants and animals provides fairly accurate estimates of the ages of samples. Carbon-14 dating techniques help climatologists determine when climate changes took place millions of years ago. Tree samples under ice masses, for example, provide a time line for glaciers. The carbon-14 content of peat and driftwood samples can also add information to the glacier chronology. In addition, temperature and climatic conditions can be inferred from radiocarbon dating of shells preserved in deep-sea sediments. As Dr. Schneider puts it, the radiocarbon dating tool has allowed climatologists "to obtain a worldwide picture of climate for about the past 40,000 years."

Climatologists also make use of isotopic analysis of ice cores. This is one of the principal methods for gathering climate information. An ice core is drilled from the Greenland ice cap, and each layer of ice— representing a year's accumulation—is analyzed for its isotopic, or oxygen-atom, composition. Oxygen is comprised of three isotopes: O16, O17, and O18. The lightest isotope is O16, which evaporates in water at a higher rate than the heavier O18. The difference in evaporation rate between O16 and O18 corresponds to the rise and fall of temperature. A depletion of O18 compared to O16 (a negative value) usually indicates a colder climate. If the ratio of O18 to O16 is higher (or positive), a warmer temperature is indicated. Thus the ratio of O16 to O18 in ice samples indicates the average temperature of a given year.

Other climatic data come from analyzing pollen grains in dry lake beds and from studying fossilized plants that grew thousands of years ago. Scientists measure the width and number of tree rings to determine age and good growth years. Some researchers study the movement of glaciers revealed by rock formations.

Documents from recent historical periods also reveal climatic events or weather conditions. Diaries, ships' logs, letters, and other written records and reports may contain descriptions of such events as storms, droughts, earthquakes, and floods. Severe winters, Invasions of pests, crop yields, and similar documentation in historical accounts can be linked to climatic patterns.

Much of the evidence related to climate still comes from secondary sources. That is, climate has not been directly observed, recorded, and then scientifically analyzed. Only in recent decades have reliable instruments been available to measure accurately—and on a global scale—such climatic variables as temperature, humidity, precipitation, and wind velocity.

CLIMATE NETWORKS

People have studied weather events and climatic patterns for centuries. In fact, our word "climate" has its roots in ancient Greece, evolving from the Greek word *klima* ("slope"). According to ancient beliefs, the earth north of the Mediterranean "sloped" away from the sun; in the south it sloped toward the sun. This sloping, the ancients thought, resulted in very cold northern temperatures and "torrid" southern climates, too hot for plant and animal life.

The Greek theory about the relation of climate to the earth's latitude was accepted until explorers in the 1400s began to sail south of the Mediterranean, discovering habitable conditions at the equator. As European explorers expanded knowledge of the earth's geography and climate, scientists in the 1500s and 1600s began to develop the basic instruments—the barometer, thermometer, and anemometer (wind speed gauge)—needed to measure and record atmospheric conditions.

By the mid-1600s, the first weather network was set up. Grand Duke Ferdinand II commissioned the manufacture of standardized thermometers and had the instruments sent to Milan, Bologna, and other Italian cities, where observers recorded temperature changes on a regular basis. However, a systematic collection of weather and climatic data on a broad scale did not begin until after 1873, when the first International Meteorological Conference was held in Vienna.

Almost another century passed before a worldwide network was established to monitor the earth's climate (although monitoring of the oceans and high latitudes of the Southern Hemisphere has been sparse). Today satellites provide global weather information, but the records have not been kept long enough to allow scientists to draw exact conclusions about climatic patterns.

In spite of fragmentary data in some areas, however, objective weather information is accumulating. Weather instruments are continually being improved, and scientists use measurements and data to create computer models that help to determine the causes of climatic change in past ages and predict how climate might fluctuate in the future.

WHY CLIMATE CHANGES

Watch any TV weather forecaster point out a satellite view of a "cloud cover" or the route of the circumpolar vortex (jet stream)—the fast-flowing westerly air— and it may seem that these and a few other factors are the only characteristics affecting climatic conditions. But even over the short term, hundreds of variables could have an effect on the global climate system, which takes in much more than the components of the atmosphere and its mechanisms.

The hydrosphere—which includes oceans, rivers, and water vapor—can be a key influence on the climate. The cryosphere—that part of the earth covered by ice and snow—and the solid surface (land and ocean beds)—called the lithosphere—are part of the climate system, as is the biosphere—all living things, including humans. Each subsystem has its own internal mechanisms, and all of the subsystems interact with one another. Thus any one or combination of these factors at a given time could bring about a climatic change.

Solar energy, which is transformed many times after reaching earth and radiating from the surface, probably has the most profound effect on climate. When the amount of solar energy reaching the earth's surface fluctuates, climate mechanisms are affected because solar heating "drives" the weather machine or the circulation pattern in the atmosphere.

Dr. Gribbin provides a simplified explanation of this convection process in *Future Weather*. He writes: "The general circulation of the atmosphere is the result of hot air rising in the tropics, and being displaced north and south of the equator as more hot air rises underneath. The displaced air cools, because it radiates heat away as infrared energy into space, and sinks at higher latitudes, where it gives up more heat to the surface of the earth in regions which do not get the benefit of tropical sunshine."

A number of complex theories have been developed to explain how solar energy affects global climate, which cannot be covered in these pages but are included in some of the publications listed as "For Further Reading" at the end of this book. Some of those studies also discuss other complex, interacting mechanisms that have an effect on climate, such as variations in albedo (the ability to reflect heat) of different earth surfaces. Dark areas—forests, for example—absorb heat, and glaciers—ice-covered areas—reflect solar energy.

The earth's elliptical orbit, or oval-shaped path, around the sun is also a factor in climatic change, as described more fully in chapter 7. Additional factors that could influence climate include volcanic eruptions that create "dust veils" in the atmosphere, blocking solar energy and causing a drop in temperature over part of the globe for a season or many months. Oceans and large rivers play a major role in climatic change, since they store and release heat and also are reservoirs for carbon dioxide that is released into the atmosphere.

Going back to the carbon dioxide question, scientists point out (as mentioned earlier) that human activities are responsible for much of the atmospheric carbon dioxide buildup, which in turn can have an effect on climate. During the past few decades, the human factor and its link to climate change have been major concerns to climatologists studying the greenhouse effect.

CHAPTER THREE

THE HUMAN FACTOR

What are the human factors that cause carbon dioxide buildup in the atmosphere? Fossil-fuel combustion, especially coal burning, and changes in land use have released carbon dioxide at an accelerated rate since the beginning of the industrial period. Human activities are also contributing to an increase in other atmospheric gases, such as nitrous oxide, methane, and chlorofluorocarbons, which are believed to contribute to a greenhouse effect.

FOSSIL FUELS

Oil, gas, coal, and oil shale from the oceans—these fossil fuels are merely preserved forms of carbon. When they are burned, carbon is emitted and combined with oxygen, forming carbon dioxide.

Measured in gigatons, or GT (giga = billion), one gigaton of burnt carbon releases about four gigatons of carbon dioxide, which flows from one "sink," or holding place, to another in the never-ending carbon cycle.

Scientists estimate that ten to thirty GT of carbon dioxide from fossil-fuel combustion will be released into the atmosphere each year during the next few decades. However, researchers have recently theorized that only about one-half of the carbon dioxide is retained in the atmosphere; the rest may return to the oceans and biota (fauna and flora of a region).

Carbon dioxide held in the atmosphere is called "the airborne fraction." If the airborne fraction remains high, more carbon dioxide emitted into the atmosphere will stay there, and climatic change is likely to occur sooner than if the airborne fraction is low.

Scientists predict that future fossil-fuel emissions will increase, thus the airborne fraction of carbon dioxide in the atmosphere will go up. The basis for such a projection is the belief that the top layers of the ocean, which serve as the primary holding place (or sink) of carbon not retained in the atmosphere, will become saturated. Although over hundreds of years the oceans can absorb most of the carbon dioxide from fossil-fuel combustion, fuels are being burned more rapidly than the ocean can take up or dissolve the compounds. In addition, if temperatures rise and the sea warms up, the ocean's capacity to absorb carbon dioxide diminishes, since carbon dioxide dissolves more effectively in cold ocean water.

CHANGES IN LAND USE

Throughout history, as human population has expanded, trees have been cut down to supply fuel, to make room for grazing animals and planting crops, and for developing urban centers. Until about 5,000 years ago, for example, when people began to harvest wood and raise goats—allowing them to graze over extensive land areas for prolonged periods—areas of the Mediterranean Basin were largely forested. Until the 1600s, vast forests also covered much of England.

Deforestation of such large geographic areas came about at a slow pace compared to the rate of change in recent history. Since the 1960s about 1.5 percent of the world's tropical forests have been cut down each year and an estimated total of 20 million acres (8 million ha) of land (including grasslands and swamps) have been cleared annually. Much of the deforestation and land disturbance takes place for agricultural purposes in the Amazon region, Malaysia, and the Soviet Union. Continual disruption and land-use changes are expected to add to the carbon dioxide accumulation in the atmosphere.

Some scientists argue, however, that increased carbon dioxide in the atmosphere may have a beneficial effect, since photosynthesis would be enhanced and plant growth would thus be stimulated. Increased growth would in turn allow plants to store additional carbon. Furthermore, as harvested or cleared areas were replanted, new trees and other biota would become sinks for carbon dioxide.

For decades scientists have debated whether the biosphere holds more carbon dioxide than it releases —or vice versa. A noted authority on the greenhouse effect, biologist George Woodwell, and his colleagues at the Marine Biological Laboratory at Woods Hole, Massachusetts, have found evidence that "seems to support the conclusion that the terrestrial biota [land plants and animals] has for many decades been a net source of carbon dioxide rather than a sink." In a 1978 report published in *Scientific American*, Dr. Woodwell said: "the destruction of the forests of the earth is adding carbon dioxide to the atmosphere at a rate comparable to the rate of release from the combustion of fossil fuels. . . ." He added that the decay of humus (fallen leaves, stalks, and other organic matter) contributes even more to the greenhouse effect, especially when land is cleared and stubble is left to decay.

OTHER "GREENHOUSE GASES"

To further complicate the factors that lead to the greenhouse effect, other trace gases—some of which are the result of human activities—are accumulating in the atmosphere. Nitrous oxide (N_2O) is an example. Most nitrous oxide and other nitrogen oxides in the air come from a biological process called denitrification—part of the nitrogen cycle in which free oxygen returns to the air. But recent measurements of nitrous oxide concentrations show a slight increase during the 1970–80 period. Scientists are not absolutely certain what the source(s) might be, but evidence points to the increased use of nitrogen fertilizers to meet the worldwide need for more food.

As the demand for food continues to increase, more nitrogen oxides will probably be produced, which could contribute to global warming. Studies published in the *Journal of Atmospheric Science* in 1980 suggest that if nitrous oxide levels double, the global temperature could rise another .5–.7° F (.3–.4° C) above the increase induced by carbon dioxide.

Nitrous oxide could also react with other atmospheric gases, leading to higher levels of ozone (gases from natural and human sources in a layer of the atmosphere that absorbs energy). Thus temperatures could rise another .2–.4° F (.1–.2° C). Yet once again there are many unknowns. Researchers must find ways to measure the natural sources and sinks of nitrous oxide before they can project future levels in the atmosphere and how climate would be affected.

Methane is another trace gas that could add a fraction of a degree to the global temperature. Although

24

methane comes from natural biological processes, such as fermentation in rice fields and swamps and in the digestive tracts of some animals, an increase in this so-called natural gas has been attributed to agricultural expansion. In nations around the globe, more rice paddies are being planted and more farm animals are being raised to meet the food demands of growing populations.

About one-half of one GT of methane has been entering the atmosphere annually, and that amount is increasing by about 2 percent per year, the EPA reports. Since methane, like nitrous oxide or carbon dioxide, absorbs infrared radiation, an increase in its concentration in the atmosphere could cause another .4–.5° F (.2–.3° C) rise in global temperature by the year 2050.

A similar effect on temperature has been linked to chlorofluorocarbons (CFCs or Freons), gases that are directly related to human activities—industrial production and certain manufactured products such as insulated packing materials and refrigeration equipment, and gas-propelled spray cans. (CFCs as propellants are now outlawed in the United States and some other countries.) CFCs are stored mainly in the oceans and also in the stratosphere, were they destroy ozone. Such an effect, some researchers theorize, might help to reduce the overall increase of greenhouse gases. But the breakdown of ozone could also lead to increased ultraviolet radiation, a potential health threat. Scientists say that projections on the amount of CFCs that are accumulating in the atmosphere would be "misleading" at this time, since bans on emissions of these gases may be more widespread in the future.

CHAPTER FOUR

CARBON DIOXIDE AND CLIMATE SCENARIOS

Climate-by-computer is an extremely important tool in the study of carbon dioxide buildup in the atmosphere. Since the 1970s researchers have been developing and refining numerical models of global climate, using a wide range of weather conditions expressed in statistics and mathematical equations. The most sophisticated computer models are "three-dimensional general circulation models" (GCMs).

GCMs take into account the general circulation of the atmosphere along with such components as variations in ocean temperature and the extent of ice masses. The results of computer calculations are compared with weather conditions that can actually be observed. Most climate models have accurately reproduced global climatic patterns.

Yet because there are so many variables—changes in solar radiation, atmospheric conditions, albedo, and vegetation, to name just a few—even the most advanced climate models cannot calculate the fine details of climatic change on a regional scale. And researchers say computer models have to be expanded to include other factors, such as cloud formations, increased water vapor from higher temperatures, and heat exchange between the oceans and the atmosphere. But the results of computer calculations do predict, on the basis of a given set of conditions, major circulation patterns, average seasonal changes, and what kind of weather is likely to occur on a large global scale in the decades ahead. Most climatologists consider the "big picture" fairly reliable, and they generally agree that there is a potential for climatic change at an unprecedented rate if carbon dioxide concentrations continue to increase in the atmosphere.

CLIMATE ANALOGUES

Researchers also look for clues about climate change in "warm-earth analogues." In other words, scientists reconstruct past climates to provide parallels for what weather could be like with global warming.

"One important advantage of this approach is that the interaction within the complex systems that determine climate can be examined as a whole," the EPA report on global warming explains, adding that there are drawbacks since the causes of warmer climates are not fully understood. When studying warm-earth analogues, scientists can only assume that "whatever forces produced the climate, the effects are similar to those caused by increases in greenhouse gases."

Nevertheless, studies of past climates help researchers to identify relationships between the "big picture" and weather conditions on a regional or local scale. Records of warm-earth periods show what kinds of climatic patterns existed and provide the basis for a scenario, or an outline, of future events.

William Kellog, at the National Center for Atmospheric Research (NCAR) in Boulder, Colorado, has conducted a number of paleoclimatic studies and has extensively examined what climatologists call the Altithermal Period, from about 4,000 to 8,000 years ago. Within that time span, climate on a global scale was warmer than it is now, which had an effect on circulation patterns similar to what might occur with an enhanced greenhouse effect.

Dr. Kellog's oft-cited 1977 study of the Altithermal, along with later work by other scientists, determined that the midsection of the North American continent was drier 4,000 to 8,000 years ago, while the subtropics were wetter than today's conditions. The studies also indicate that there was more overall precipitation during the Altithermal than there is now, but most of it probably fell into the oceans and on coastal areas. The increased moisture may have been due to the warming of the poles and the equator. The contrast in temperatures between the poles and equator is the force that moves high-level winds, so a reduced contrast probably produced weaker winds that would not have pushed storms very far inland.

Another scientist, Herman Flohn, at the International Institute for Applied Systems Analysis in Austria, has studied the climate of the geologic periods 120,000 and 10,000,000 years ago and the climate of the Middle Ages, about 1,000 years ago. Using a variety of paleoclimatic techniques, Flohn concluded that global temperatures ranged 4.5–7° F (2.5–4° C) higher in the respective geologic periods and 33° F (1° C) higher in the Middle Ages.

Because of these warmer climates, living conditions in the Northern Hemisphere were very different from those existing now. During the Middle Ages, for instance, trees grew farther north in Canada and Europe, and the European continent suffered frequent dry spells. Grapevines grew in England, where climate does not now support such a crop. At the same time, the Vikings established thriving farm settlements in areas of Greenland that are now too cold and harsh to attract many inhabitants.

RECENT HISTORICAL PATTERNS

In the search for a historical climate that would be parallel to the contemporary warming trend, meteorologist Harold Bernard, Jr., in his book *The Greenhouse Effect*, refers to a more recent past, the 1930s. He says that decade "marked the peak of the most recent global warming," and he describes the 1930s as "years of sweltering heat waves, earth-cracking droughts, and maximum tropical storm frequency." High temperatures and droughts plagued the Midwest in the United States, parts of Russia, and southern Australia. Along with the warming climate, the ocean temperatures rose, and various species of fish usually found in southern waters migrated much farther north than would be expected with today's climate, Bernard says.

The average temperature for the 1930s was 1° F (fraction of a degree Celsius) warmer than in the past decades. But just adding a slight increase to present temperatures does not provide an analogy for future climate. As Bernard points out, "Records from specific areas must be analysed in detail to determine how the varying atmospheric circulation patterns affected different regions." He believes weather records from the 1930s show what we can expect if there is a global warming: a possible return of the "dust bowl" in the United States—that is, severe droughts across the midsection of the nation. Along with a warming trend, Bernard predicts a change in the westerlies and an increase in hurricane strikes and tornadoes.

Whether warm-earth analogues reconstruct recent historical patterns or those of geologic periods millions of years ago, no one can be certain that they are close parallels to climate changes brought on by carbon dioxide. Thus climatologists stress that the analogs cannot predict how greenhouse gases will affect regional climate but merely provide guidelines for possible changes.

The same can be said for computer models of changing climate. Since the naturally interacting systems that affect climate are so complex, no valid method has yet been devised to actually measure the carbon dioxide "signal"—that is, to identify the exact cause-and-effect mechanism of this greenhouse gas. The changing composition of the atmosphere cannot be put into test tubes or examined under controlled conditions in a laboratory. Research scientist Roger Revelle and his colleague H. E. Seuss pointed this out several decades ago in a much-quoted statement: "Human beings are now carrying out a large-scale geophysical experiment of a kind that could not have happened in the past nor be repeated in the future. Within a few centuries we are returning to the atmosphere and the oceans the concentrated organic carbon stored in the sedimentary rocks over hundreds of millions of years. This experiment, if adequately documented, may yield a far-reaching insight into processes determining weather and climate. . . ."

In a recent magazine interview, Dr. Revelle repeated his earlier observation, adding that "the changes are going to happen slowly, almost imperceptibly from year to year, but it's not too soon to begin planning how to make use of them."

ANOTHER VIEW

Sherman B. Idso, a physicist with the United States Department of Agriculture (USDA), and Reginald E. Newell at the Massachusetts Institute of Technology, along with a few other researchers, have attempted to show that the global warming induced by a doubling of atmospheric carbon dioxide would be much less than predicted by most major climate models. Idso, for example, claims that global temperatures would increase by less than a quarter of a degree. He also believes a two- to threefold increase in carbon dioxide would be desirable since this would bring about a 20–50 percent increase in agricultural production (due to increased photosynthesis).

However, the report of the National Research Council panel, which assessed carbon dioxide effects, found the Idso studies "incomplete and misleading." Published by the NAS, the report points out that Idso and others who have reached similar conclusions have not taken into account various processes that bring about a global warming due to the greenhouse effect.

Climatologist Stephen Schneider agrees, writing in his 1984 study *The Coevolution of Climate and Life:* "In my opinion, it has been convincingly shown that the neglect of horizontal heat flow between land and sea, omission of heat storage in the air and oceans, and failure to account for total atmosphere/surface energy budget have caused Newell's and Idso's low estimates" of global warming due to carbon dioxide doubling.

CHANGES VARY BY REGION

If global temperatures increased 35–37° F (2–3° C) because carbon dioxide concentration doubled, this higher temperature would not be reflected evenly around the earth. Studies show that temperatures would be higher in polar and subpolar regions due to feedback mechanisms. In climatology the feedback processes are those, such as developing cloud cover and increased water vapor in the atmosphere, that modify weather conditions. In his recent study, Schneider presents this example of one way the process works:

> Suppose a warm wind blows over a valley covered lightly with snow. The temperature will rise, of course, melting the snow cover and replacing a bright, highly reflective snow surface with a much darker, more sunlight-absorbing meadow. Thus, the temperature rise caused initially by the warm wind will be further enhanced by the positive-feedback effect on temperature of disappearing snow cover. Similarly, a cold snap that brings on a snow cover tends to reduce the amount of solar heat absorbed . . . thereby intensifying the cold.

Studies vary, but a 5° F (3° C) increase in global temperatures is expected to result in a rise of possibly 13–18 or 18–22° F (7–10 or 10–12° C) at the poles due in part to such feedback mechanisms as melting ice and surface albedo. At the equator, the temperature would rise no more than 5° F (3° C). Since the temperature difference between the poles and the equator is the force that drives high-level winds on the planet, a much greater differential would probably mean that warm tropical air would be transported toward the poles. Such an effect would alter other regions as well.

How would present regional weather change? That is the big question. Since a temperature increase alone says little about climatic change, climatologists can only suggest that frost-free regions of the world would expand and precipitation patterns would probably change greatly.

Most climate models indicate that there would be reduced rainfall and snow across the latitudes that include the United States. At higher latitudes—in Canada and Siberia, for example—there is likely to be increased precipitation and a longer growing season. At lower latitudes, too, south of the United States, increased rainfall is expected.

Such changes would have a tremendous impact on agriculture worldwide. A global warming and increased precipitation could bring economic benefits to some countries now considered "poor" by North American standards. At the same time, sections of the Northern Hemisphere could be adversely affected if agricultural productivity drops. Thus the effects on agriculture are one of the major concerns of climatologists studying carbon dioxide buildup.

CHAPTER FIVE

EFFECTS ON AGRICULTURE AND WATER SUPPLIES

An expected global temperature increase of 4–5° F (2–3° C) by the middle of the next century would not by itself make a big difference in world agricultural production. But changes in agriculture are likely because of alterations in precipitation patterns and the effects on water supply and distribution. Shifts in dry and wet regions of the earth could bring about changes not only in where certain crops are grown but also in where food animals are raised. Even the types of pests and weeds that destroy crops could be altered by a warming trend and changes in moisture levels.

Agricultural impacts from a greenhouse warming would probably be felt most severely in North America, particularly in the United States, many researchers say. Almost all of the U.S. food supply comes from crops and food animals raised on one-third of a billion acres (33 million hectares). Some of the major U.S. crops also feed millions of people in other nations. Almost half of the U.S. production of corn and wheat, for example, goes to world markets. Any significant drop in the yield of corn and wheat plus soybeans (the three most valuable U.S. agricultural products) could have a detrimental effect on the nation's economy as well as create food shortages on a global scale.

ALTERED CROP PRODUCTION

"American crops growing from 35 to 49 degrees latitude are within the zone that meteorologists predict will experience a change in the weather as CO_2 increases," research scientist Paul Waggoner of the Connecticut Agricultural Experiment Station writes in the NRC's carbon dioxide report. With warmer and drier climate expected in America's major growing zone, Dr. Waggoner and other scientists have calculated that such weather changes "will decrease yields of the three great American food crops (soybeans, wheat, and corn) over the entire grain belt by 5 to 10 percent." This reduction would come about even though there is the probability of increased plant growth due to expanded photosynthesis.

Waggoner is careful to point out, however, that agricultural changes caused by weather fluctuations "are too complex to be distilled into a few statistics." He points out that throughout history, alterations in rain, snow, temperature, and wind patterns and general atmospheric changes have affected agriculture and population in a variety of ways.

Extreme weather changes have at times destroyed some types of crops. And an increase in pests, weeds, and related problems can make the effects of bad weather even worse. Drastic weather changes have often forced people to move to more habitable environments. Other groups of people have been able to adapt farming practices to fit the changing climate. Some civilizations have been weakened by climate-induced changes in agriculture.

Waggoner draws an example from ancient Rome. "When rain fell abundantly on Italy from 450 to 250 B.C., intensive agriculture was fruitful and the Roman

36

Republic was vigorous," he writes. Another period of Roman prosperity accompanied the plentiful rains that fell from 100 B.C. to 50 A.D. But rainfall began to decrease after 80 A.D., and grains could no longer be produced in large enough yields to feed the growing population. The people adapted to the changing climate by planting grapevines and olive trees. But these crops were not sufficient to maintain an expanding civilization. Although a changing agriculture was not the only factor in the decline of the Roman Empire, the loss of grain crops contributed to the nation's collapse.

Weather-related impacts on agriculture can be linked to other catastrophic periods in history. Colder climate and excessive rainfall during the first half of the 1300s brought shorter growing seasons and floods. Crops failed, and famine and disease spread across Europe.

Droughts affected North American agriculture during the late 1800s. Wheat crops failed across the grain belt of the United States. And winter snowstorms in the Dakotas froze great herds of cattle.

The U.S. dust bowl of the 1930s has already been mentioned. But along with the dry weather came an invasion of weeds and such pests as grasshoppers, which destroyed over $100 million in crops during a single year.

FUTURE AGRICULTURAL SHIFTS

Past weather changes and their impact on agriculture provide some clues for the future. According to warm-earth analogues, there will be both winners and losers in a greenhouse-warmed earth.

Walter Orr Roberts, retired director of the NCAR and president emeritus of the University Corporation that manages the NCAR, says that eastern Africa would be one of the winners. In a recent interview Dr. Roberts noted that a global warming could bring about a twofold increase in rainfall in eastern Africa. Although not a large increase for that part of the world, a doubling in rainfall "would have an enormously beneficial effect on the lower reaches of Ethiopia's great river, the Awash." It would then be possible to increase food production in the river basin. Robert emphasized, however, that the potential is already there for better crop yields, but wars and other strife have hampered production. Still, with climate changes brought on by a warming trend—and with better management—Roberts believes Africa could "produce enough food for all its people."

Roger Revelle, a well-known authority on greenhouse effects, agrees. Dr. Revelle has also pointed out that the Ganges Plain in India as well as the Sudan in Africa could be world breadbaskets as a result of rising global temperatures and increased rainfall.

When it comes to losers, most scientists studying greenhouse effects conclude that the "richer" areas of the world will suffer most. The greatest agricultural impacts may well be on the United States and Canada. As Dr. Roberts explains it: "Some parts of Canada might become warm enough to encourage an increase in production. A 1 degree Celsius rise lengthens the growing season about a week, so southern Canada might get an additional three weeks between first and last frost. But the overall loss of moisture might more than counter that gain."

For the United States, Roberts can see few benefits. During his interview, he noted:

The Sorghum Belt will move north into the corn-growing region, and the Corn Belt will have to shift maybe 300 miles northward, where the land is less productive. Furthermore, though sorghum and soybeans aren't extremely sensitive to July heat, a brief spell of very hot weather during the tassel season can do great harm to the corn crop. The approximately 25 percent yield loss in 1983 resulted from just a short spell of extreme heat during the sensitive period.

Since the United States exports a large portion of its grain to the Soviet Union, any discussion of agricultural impacts brought on by greenhouse warming always includes questions about Russia's food supply. Many biologists, climatologists, and other scientists expect the Soviet Union to produce more grain in the years ahead, reducing much of its imports from the United States and other countries.

EFFECTS ON WATER SUPPLIES

Although a global warming trend could result in less rainfall for the USSR, the Soviets may still be able to increase grain production because of available water supplies. Vast irrigation systems are being developed, and plans are being made to divert the Orb and Yinesy rivers to farming areas. Just half the flow of the Orb River, if diverted, could irrigate a region the size of France.

In other parts of the world, however, if a drier climate prevails, water resources might not be so accessible. Studies show, for example, that just a slight decrease in precipitation along with warmer temperatures could severely affect water resources in seven western water regions of the United States, or almost half the nation. Based on a 10 percent reduction in precipitation and a global warming of 4° F (2° C), water supplies by the year 2000 are expected to diminish from 40 to almost 76 percent, with the Rio Grande area the hardest hit.

Except for the Pacific Northwest and the Great Basin (parts of Nevada, Idaho, and Utah), the greatest water consumption in western states at present is for irrigation purposes. One out of seven acres (2.8 hectares) of American cropland is irrigated, with most of that acreage in the western half of the United States. The irrigation water comes from streams and underground sources that in turn are supplied by runoff from precipitation (for example, snowmelts in mountain areas). Thus, if precipitation declines, runoff is reduced and water supplies for irrigation are diminished.

To prevent agricultural losses because of diminished irrigation, water can be transferred or diverted from one river basin to another in some western states. Such is already the case in Southern California. In fact, California now receives about 15 percent of its water supply from the Colorado River, and much of that supply sustains agriculture in the dry southern region. Obviously, water shortages could seriously affect the production of valuable crops that are grown in Southern California and shipped to many parts of the nation and the world.

Water shortages could also be felt in the vast central plains of the United States, which depend on an underground reservoir—actually a subsurface lake— for irrigation of grainfields. Known as the Ogallala Aquifer, the reservoir spans an area from South Dakota to northern Texas, and water is pumped to the surface for agricultural use. The problem is that heavy consumption has already reduced the water level of the reservoir. Meteorologist Harold Bernard notes that the water table has been falling at a rate of 2 to 7 feet (61 to 213 cm) per year, causing thousands of wells to dry up and many farmers to revert to dryland operations or to give up farming altogether.

According to a number of studies, including one by the U.S. National Academy of Sciences, with continued tapping of underground water sources and an increase in dryland cultivation, there is little doubt that agricultural production will suffer. In addition, the rapid consumption of underground water in the Central Plains will make the region more vulnerable to increased summer dryness due to the greenhouse effect. As climatologist Stephen Schneider put it: "We may be prematurely using up the very irrigation source that will be needed to help us adapt to a new and potentially drier Central Plains."

ADAPTING U.S. AGRICULTURE

A number of researchers are convinced that agriculture in the United States can be adapted to a warmer and drier climate, despite predictions of lower crop production in many regions. History shows that farmers have not ignored weather changes, and that they have altered their practices over the years as crop yields have fallen. Paul Waggoner explains it this way in the NRC report:

> If the climate changes, farmers will move themselves, change crops, modify varieties, and alter husbandry. The loss of cropland to the margins of the desert, for example, may be replaced in the national production by higher yields and more cropland at the frigid margins. Seeking higher yields and more profit, they will correct their course annually, and they may even adapt to a slowly changing climate unconsciously and successfully.

One of the ways farmers adapt their agricultural methods is by planting new seeds that have been developed to survive in a changing environment. Plant breeding and testing is a continual process in the United States and in a number of European countries where experiment stations are maintained. Developing new plants and seeds involves not only adapting crops to weather conditions but also learning what mechanisms plants use to resist stress (such as cold or drought) and to produce higher yields. Such processes, although lengthy, are some insurance against great declines in crop yields.

Increasing water storage will be another method used to reduce the effects of a warmer and drier climate. Farmers already rotate crops or allow soil to lie fallow (without planting) so that moisture can build up. Land can be terraced or leveled to prevent water runoff. Studies show that more efficient irrigation— diverting water only to areas where it is needed— could save water resources significantly. More productive plants and pest control also help to conserve water use.

Climatic change may force some forms of agriculture into different regions of the nation. Moving the grain-growing belts northward is one example. If water shortages cause irrigated croplands to dry up in the Southwest, vegetable and fruit crops might have to be cultivated elsewhere. More fresh produce may have to be grown on the Atlantic Coast, where large commercial vegetable crops were once produced but declined after midcentury with westward migrations.

If such adaptations take place, researchers see very little change in the total yield of agricultural crops in the United States by the year 2000. Scientists suggest that grains and other life-sustaining crops will be developed to grow in warmer and drier climates.

EFFECTS ON LESS-DEVELOPED COUNTRIES

While highly mobile, industrialized nations, such as the United States and Canada, may be able to adapt their agricultural practices to thrive in a greenhouse warming, what happens in less-developed countries? Those that are not now self-sufficient in terms of food supplies may lack the funds, technology, and even the will to make far-reaching changes in farming practices. In many Third World nations—the developing countries of Africa, Asia, and parts of South America —people are more concerned about how to import food aid for day-to-day survival.

Yet, as John Gribbin maintains, "immediate increases in food production could be achieved in many of the poorest, hungriest regions of the world" if better farming methods were employed, such as conservation of moisture by terracing and addition of natural fertilizers like compost and manure to the soil. But most Third World farmers have little incentive to increase their crop yields, since the benefits go to a small number of wealthy landowners, not to the millions of peasants who work the soil and produce the food. Most peasants rent land and are deeply in debt for seed, fertilizer, tools, and other resources needed for farming. Landownership would have to be more widespread before large numbers of farmers would take the initiative to boost agricultural production.

Even if climatic changes due to greenhouse effects create more favorable agricultural conditions for poorer nations, bringing about changes in agricultural practices may be difficult. Farming systems are very closely tied to a region's culture or way of life, and people tend to resist changes in traditional patterns of living. Also, the communication and transportation systems and other means of distributing food beyond local growing areas do not exist and are too costly to develop.

In addition to cultural resistance to agricultural changes and lack of marketing networks, some governments refuse to revamp policies that stand in the way of improved food production. A country might have a national policy, for example, that encourages raising crops that can be exported for income rather than encouraging production of crops to feed the population. In such instances, more than enough food might be raised to provide for the needs of the population, but it will be exported in order to pay for manufactured goods or fossil fuels such as oil and coal.

A changing climate, then, is only one of the many concerns in areas of the world where people have barely enough food to survive. But these problems could become more severe if food-growing patterns are altered on a warmer earth. Those who can adapt will probably do so. Those who cannot help themselves may resort to force in order to obtain food and other supplies for survival. Because of these possibilities, some scientists believe that more of the wealthy nations' resources need to be used to improve agriculture on a global scale, rather than launching expensive programs to combat the carbon dioxide buildup. Worldwide improvements in agriculture could ensure against adverse impacts of many types of climate changes, not just those that will accompany a greenhouse warming.

CHAPTER SIX

THE RISING SEA LEVEL

According to some studies, another expected impact of global warming is a substantial rise in sea level during the years ahead. Such a theory suggests that increased temperatures due to the buildup of greenhouse gases will cause ice and snow to melt and run off into the oceans. The oceans could also expand thermally—that is, warming would reduce the water density and increase volume. Thermal expansion and runoff would raise water levels, although there are many different estimates on the extent of such a rise.

On the other hand, analyses presented at a recent American Geophysical Union conference indicate that the sea level might stay the same or even drop due to global warming. This theory is based in part on a projected carbon dioxide buildup that is 50 percent less than most computer models have shown so far. Such a projection was made by Richard Somerville, a meteorologist with the Scripps Institute of Oceanography, whose studies take into account the effects of clouds. If warming occurs, clouds will accumulate, becoming wetter and more dense because of increased evaporation. Denser clouds will reflect more solar energy, which in turn could slow down the warming trend.

Another study presented at the conference suggests that increased evaporation is leading to an accumulation of ice in the Antarctic. Apparently the increasing ice comes from ocean water that evaporates and falls as snow. According to Mark Meier, a glaciologist with the U.S. Geological Survey, the current rate of ice buildup could lower the sea level as much as half a millimeter annually.

WHAT IF THE SEA LEVEL RISES?

Obviously, there is a great deal of controversy about warming temperatures and their effect on the sea level. A few glaciologists are concerned not about ice buildup but the breakup of large ice sheets in West Antarctica. These glaciers extend from the land far out over the sea and are now stationary because ice shelves hold them in place. If the earth warms, the ice shelves could melt away or weaken, causing ice sheets to break away into the ocean.

Melting and breakup of the West Antarctic ice could occur within the next century if polar warming due to an increased greenhouse effect becomes greater than the average global increase. According to some estimates, the sea level could rise up to 20 feet (5–6 m) if the West Antarctic ice sheets melt. However, most studies indicate that such a rise would not occur very rapidly and it would in fact take place over several hundred years.

Even though a great "ice surge" might not materialize, scientists continue to explore the possibilities of sea level rise and its effects. Shorelines, for example, could erode and lowlands could be covered by water. If sea levels should rise to heights of 20 feet (6 meters) or so, much of the east coast of the United States, including most of Florida, the coastal areas around the Gulf of Mexico, and some parts of the west coast would be under water. In fact, many major cities and ports worldwide would be inundated.

Another impact of sea-level rise would be the intrusion of salt water into rivers, streams, and groundwater sources. If salt water moves into freshwater sources, entire ecosystems could be altered. Drinking water supplies could also be reduced. And alteration of freshwater systems plus flooding could have adverse effects on agricultural production.

PLANNING FOR
SEA LEVEL RISE

There seems little doubt that if the sea level continues to rise, economic losses would be severe in many parts of the world and millions of people would be displaced and suffer hardships. But any impacts would depend on how well people had planned for the physical changes that would be brought about by sea-level rise. Businesses, governments, and individuals in coastal and low-lying areas would have to prepare for such effects as erosion and flooding.

For example, plans would have to be set up for evacuating people living in low-lying areas in danger of imminent flooding. Hazardous-waste sites, power stations, and utilities might have to be relocated. If new roads, bridges, parks, factories, housing, and many other facilities are going to be built, decisions would have to be made on how close to the sea to locate such public and private developments. Possibly some buildings would have to be constructed on piers or landfills. More seawalls, dams, and levees might be needed.

The recent NRC report, *Changing Climate*, underscores the need for setting up such "defenses" against the "threat" of high sea water. Thomas C.

Schelling of Harvard University points out that the Netherlands has long adapted to such conditions with dikes or levees. More than 7 million Dutch live below sea level, and the country has found it cost-effective to protect the land from high seas.

Dr. Schelling explains how the economics of building dikes would apply in an east coast area of the United States, where a 5 meter (16 ft) rise in the sea

> would cover most of downtown Boston. Beacon Hill, containing the State House, would be an island separated by about 1.9 miles (3 km) from the nearest mainland. Most of adjacent Cambridge would be awash. But it would take only 2.5 miles (4 km) of dikes, mostly built on land that is currently above sea level, to defend the entire area. Perhaps even more economical, because it would avoid the political costs of choosing what to save and what to give up and of condemning land for right-of-way, would be a dike 8 or 10 km in length to enclose all of Boston Harbor.

In addition to dikes, Schelling suggests building new deepwater port facilities outside the enclosed harbor and diverting rivers. He notes that no realistic estimates on the costs of such a plan have been made, but he believes the cost of defense would be much less than the replacement costs for the land and facilities that would be lost.

Yet, Schelling says, the situation would be "totally different for an area like the coast of Bangladesh" (a country in southern Asia, formerly a province of Pakistan). The area is subject to flooding from the sea, as borne out by the recent flood, and also from inland rivers. Unlike Boston, there is no "concentration of capital assets that can be enclosed by a few miles of dikes . . . the levees required to protect the country would be many times greater than the length of the shoreline."

Thus defense is not always a practical solution for sea-level rise. In some cases, people may have to gradually retreat from coastal areas. Urban centers may have to be relocated.

MORE RESEARCH

So far only a few research projects have been undertaken in the United States to estimate the physical and economic effects of rising sea level. The EPA has provided funds for studies on the impact of sea-level rise for areas around Charleston, South Carolina, and Galveston, Texas. And researchers have concluded that "a 1.5 meter [5-ft] rise in sea level would inundate one-quarter of Charleston if no additional bulkheads or seawalls were constructed . . . [and] areas in Charleston that are now flooded once every 100 years would be flooded once every 10 years." The Galveston area would not be quite as vulnerable to land loss, the studies show, especially if "the existing network of levees and seawalls were maintained," the EPA says.

Some research is underway by civil engineers and geologists to determine what kinds of port and coastal structures are needed to withstand a sea-level rise along the east coast and what effects such a rise would have on drinking water. But there is a need for additional research and cooperative planning, involving zoning officials, architects, geologists, paleoclimatologists, and people in many other disciplines. As the EPA has pointed out, half the damage from sea-level rise can be prevented if there is adequate planning.

CHAPTER SEVEN

ICE AGE VS. ICE MELT

During the latter part of the 1970s, bitter cold winters and record snowfalls were the subject of many news stories and prompted articles on a new ice age with advancing glaciers. If, as most scientists concur, an ice age is on the way, why is there so much concern about a global warming? Won't the earth's thermal blanket be a protection against a "big freeze"?

Before such questions can be considered, scientists have had to determine just what an ice age is and when glaciations (periods when ice covers advance over the earth) have occurred. Although beginning and ending dates for glacial periods are only approximate, there is general agreement that the earth has gone through several major ice epochs. Within these major ice epochs there have been fluctuations in the climate. Individual ice ages, or glacial eras, have come and gone. That is, at times the cold has been more intense than during an interglacial or postglacial period of warming, such as the earth is now experiencing.

THE GREAT ICE AGE

The last major advance of ice over a large portion of the earth began about 25,000 to 30,000 years ago and ended about 10,000 to 14,000 years ago (although a minor advance called the Little Ice Age occurred between 1550–1850). At the height of the last glacial era, some 18,000 to 20,000 years ago, 30 percent of the earth's land (an estimated 17.5 million square miles or 45 million square kilometers) was covered with ice. Most of North America, including all of Canada and much of what is now the United States as far south as the Ohio and Missouri River valleys, was glaciated. Ice sheets also buried Scandinavia, England, and parts of Germany and Russia. Smaller ice caps spread over parts of the Southern Hemisphere, covering mountainous areas in Australia, Argentina, and even high mountain tops in Africa and Hawaii.

Some of the glaciers were thousands of feet thick and left their mark on land surfaces. Often the weight and pressure of the ice depressed land areas, and moving ice carried large boulders and great volumes of sediment from polar regions to lower latitudes or from mountains to lower levels. Evidence of ice floes has been found in many parts of the world.

During this period of vast glacial advances—often called the Great Ice Age—water was drawn from the oceans in the precipitation cycle to create the huge glaciers, and over thousands of years the sea level fell by hundreds of feet, leaving dry earth and connecting continents. A land bridge was formed from Asia to North America. Animals and people could migrate from one continent to another. Some people moved from northern regions, in search of more hospitable climate and land areas, to regions in South America.

When the earth began to warm again, the ice sheets

retreated, but not all at once. There were alternate warming and cooling periods—glaciers melted, advanced again, retreated, and so on for thousands of years until today, with Greenland and Antarctica being the primary areas of ice concentrations.

ICE AGE THEORIES

How and why warming and cooling periods come and go have been the focus of many scientific debates. As yet, there is no universally accepted explanation for what brings on an ice age. But paleoclimatologists, geologists, geophysicists, astronomers, and other scientists have developed a number of different theories to show how an ice age might be triggered.

Some studies have suggested that volcanic eruptions blast enough ash into the air to block solar energy and thus bring on a colder climate. Other theories have developed around the idea that carbon dioxide in the atmosphere is reduced, thereby allowing heat to radiate into space rather than be held in the atmosphere. Movement of the continents—the continental-drift theory, as described in chapter 2—is one other explanation for the cause of an ice age.

One of the most readable accounts of various ice-age theories is included in *Ice Ages: Solving the Mystery* by oceanographer John Imbrie and his daughter, science writer Katherine Imbrie. Dr. Imbrie was one of the principal scientists working on a ten-year program to study past climates, particularly the peak of the last ice age. Called CLIMAP (an acronym for Climate: Long-range Investigation, Mapping, and Prediction), the program was set up in 1971 by the National Science Foundation. As part of the study, scientists analyzed sediment cores from the Indian Ocean, which provided evidence of nearly 500,000 years of the earth's history. Such analysis led to the

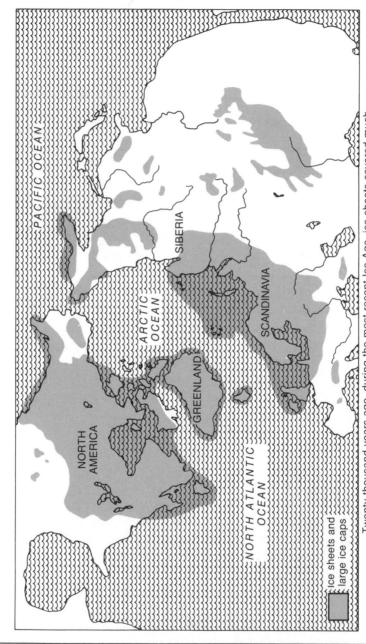

Twenty thousand years ago, during the most recent Ice Age, ice sheets covered much of North America and parts of northern Europe and Asia.

PACIFIC OCEAN

SIBERIA

ARCTIC OCEAN

SCANDINAVIA

GREENLAND

NORTH AMERICA

NORTH ATLANTIC OCEAN

Ice sheets and large ice caps

development of a map showing ice coverage during the last glacial period and helped support an astronomical theory of the ice ages. (See page 54.)

Briefly, the theory holds that the orbit and tilt of the earth bring on climate changes. First formulated by Serbian astronomer-physicist Milutin Milankovich, who began publishing his ideas in the 1920s, the theory takes into account the three orbital cycles of the earth.

One cycle involves the earth's orbit around the sun, which follows a changing path from an elongated circular pattern—an oval, or ellipse—to a nearly perfect circle. Each complete orbit of the earth marks a year's time on our calendar, but the pattern, or path, of the orbit changes from a more circular to a more flattened shape over a period of 100,000 years. The more elongated the path, the more variations there are in the distance from the sun, which in turn creates greater seasonal differences.

Another cycle involves the tilt of the earth in relation to the sun. If there were a line or plane joining the sun and earth, the earth's axis would sometimes be more upright, or perpendicular, to the sun's radiation than at others. The angle of tilt varies from about 22 degrees to about 24.5 degrees less than a right angle (90 degrees) over a period of 41,000 years. At present, the tilt is decreasing, which could prompt an ice age, since the minimum tilt brings fewer seasonal variations and helps to build up glaciers in the polar regions. (Just the opposite is true during maximum tilt, when increased solar radiation melts polar ice.)

As the earth orbits, it spins on its axis—an imaginary line connecting the North and South poles—and moves along its path in a wobbly fashion, much like a top would spin on a flat surface. As a result, the earth is closer to the sun at some times of the year and farther away at others. Dr. Gribbin explains in *Future*

Weather that "the North Pole does not 'point' always in the same direction, but moves around a circle in space, so that the imaginary line joining the North and South poles traces out a cone. . . ." This movement, called the "circle of precession," or the "precession of equinoxes," takes about 22,000 years to complete, and it very slowly changes the pattern of the seasons.

All three of these orbital elements have an effect on the amount of solar radiation reaching the earth at certain latitudes during the different seasons. Investigations by Imbrie and other scientists with the CLIMAP project have revealed that variations in orbital cycles and solar radiation apparently lead to the advance and retreat of glaciers. In fact, CLIMAP studies show that the earth's past climatic cycles match the orbital rhythms. Imbrie summed it up this way:

> Three million years ago, continental ice sheets appeared for the first time in the northern hemisphere, where they occupied areas adjacent to the North Atlantic Ocean. Apparently, once the ice sheets in this hemisphere formed, they were sensitive to astronomical variations—and they began a long and complex series of fluctuations . . . cycles of 100,000 years, 41,000 years, and about 22,000 years are clearly stamped on the climatic record of the most recent half-million years. It is these cycles that are explained by the astronomical theory of the ice ages.

A "NORMAL" CLIMATE?

Many scientists now accept the theory that orbital changes are the major cause of climatic variations. In addition, there is general acceptance that the shift of continents and their present positions also contribute to climatic conditions. In brief, the earth is at present in a position and orbital pattern that bring on "normally" cold temperatures, but a warming period prevails.

Will the warming period soon end or continue for thousands of years? Some scientists believe the peak years of warmth are over, and that the earth is on its way to the next ice age. But no one can say with any certainty when that period will begin. A few studies show a rapid approach—due to the earth's orbit and tilt—to a full ice age. Other studies suggest that the weather for the next one or two thousand years could be similar to what has been experienced in the past, except for climatic changes due to greenhouse warming. About the only general agreement concerning a coming ice age is that it will occur and probably last for many thousands of years before another interglacial comes about.

CHAPTER EIGHT

ENERGY DEMANDS AND THE GREENHOUSE WARMING

Although it is possible that a global cooling trend could mitigate any warming caused by a buildup of greenhouse gases in the atmosphere, most climatologists expect just the opposite effect in the decades ahead. Scientists are also fairly certain that much of the increase in atmospheric carbon dioxide and other trace gases is due in part to the combustion of fossil fuels to meet energy demands. Thus projections on future climatic changes are partially based on estimates of worldwide consumption of fossil fuels.

GLOBAL ENERGY DEMANDS

How do scientists determine energy demands? How do those demands contribute to carbon dioxide accumulations? Once again, computerized models have been used to develop scenarios. Some of the data input has included estimates of population and productivity, fuel costs and their relationship to demand, carbon dioxide emission rates, and improvements in energy efficiency.

One computer model developed by the Institute for

Energy Analysis (IEA) divides the world into nine regions and takes into account a number of variables for each region, such as population, productivity, and enhanced energy efficiency on the positive side and energy prices on the negative side. These factors, along with the economy of each region, help to determine the underlying demand for certain fuels and the resultant carbon dioxide emissions.

Other computer models, as mentioned in earlier chapters, determine the levels of carbon dioxide retained in the atmosphere and in other reservoirs such as the ocean. Energy scenarios also compare carbon dioxide emissions for different combinations of fuels. For example, one study shows that if industrialized nations depend primarily on nuclear energy in the years ahead, there will be only a very small rise in temperatures due to an increased greenhouse effect. On the other hand, a heavy worldwide dependence on fossil fuels would result in a rapid buildup of greenhouse gases and a dramatic increase in global temperatures.

To project carbon dioxide emissions, scientists must estimate the balance between carbon and noncarbon fuels that will be used in the future. The "fuel mix" is highly uncertain, however. No one knows exactly what types of fuels will be available and how technological changes might affect energy demands just a few decades from now. Some studies suggest that from 10 to 13 percent of the fuels used by the middle of the next century will be nonfossil. But other estimates put the nonfossil energy sources at 25 to 35 percent of the total fuel supplies.

FOSSIL FUEL SOURCES

All nations are heavily dependent on such fossil fuels as coal and oil. Other widely used fossil fuels are methane gas, methanol, and gasohol—synthetic fuels often called "synfuels," produced from coal, organic wastes such as garbage, and from grains and other plants grown on so-called energy farms.

Oil shale is another form of fossil fuel that comes from marine (underwater) and mountainous rocks deposited underwater eons ago. The deposits are widely distributed around the world, although two-thirds of the supply is in North America. But oil shale has to be mined, crushed, and heated in order to extract the oil, which is then refined to produce gasoline and other petroleum products.

Similar problems apply to oil from bituminous sands or tar sands. Such sands are filled with bitumen, a substance that produces crude oil, but the recovery process, as with oil from shale, is much more costly compared with drilling and pumping "black gold" from the earth.

RENEWABLE ENERGY SOURCES

As the nonrenewable energy supplies from fossil fuels become more expensive and difficult to obtain, more and more attention will be given to renewable sources of energy. Wind power, for example, is being explored in various parts of the United States. Electricity is generated by windmills—not the old-fashioned kind that pump water from wells in rural areas, but high-technology structures that look like huge aircraft propellers atop towers as high as 100 feet (30 meters).

Another form of energy that can help cut back on fossil-fuel use is solar power, which is being developed in many parts of the world. Of course, the sun's energy has always been available for human use through green plants, which convert solar energy during the process of photosynthesis. Since the decayed organic matter once consumed the sun's radiation, fossil fuels are a form of stored solar energy. Wind power and hydroelectric power are also generated in part by solar energy, the driving force behind air and water movement.

Yet the sun's energy can be harnessed more directly for human use. A number of research projects are underway to find practical and economical methods to produce photovoltaic (PV) power—that is, to collect radiation from the sun in solar cells that convert the energy to electricity.

How do such systems work? Solar cells, made from silicon, are formed into disks or rectangles with grids (tiny conducting lines) attached. Atoms in the silicon absorb sunshine, which releases electrons. The free electrons then collect on one surface of the cell and complete a circuit along the metal grid lines, creating an electrical current. When many cells are connected, as in flat panels on rooftops, the electricity generated can heat or cool a building.

In the United States, a number of homes, schools, and other structures are being heated and cooled by solar energy, but backup systems using conventional fuels are needed during bad weather and in snowbelt areas, where the sun is often obscured during winter months.

The production (and storage) of PV power on a mass scale would have a great impact on energy demands, since 35 to 39 percent of the primary energy supplies used in the United States, Japan, and Canada generate electricity. By the year 2000, industrialized nations are expected to use 45 percent of their energy supplies for electrical power, with the less-developed countries following close behind.

Geothermal energy is another renewable source of power. Basically, the process involves "tapping" underground steam that comes from natural sources such as hot springs and geysers. Some electrical power is being generated now in western areas of the United States and in Iceland, where steam escapes continually from the earth. In other instances electrical power could be generated from geothermal plants set up in hot, dry regions. Scientific experiments have shown that water can be pumped into the hot inner earth and that the pressure from the water would crack rocks thousands of feet below the surface. In this way the water would be heated, forming steam, which would be piped to a generating station above ground. (See illustration on page 64.)

Energy may also come from the ocean. Over 70 percent of the earth's surface is covered by water— oceans and seas that store huge amounts of solar energy. Ocean Thermal Energy Conversion (OTEC) power plants are being developed to generate electricity through a process that makes use of the temperature difference between warm surface waters and deep, cold ocean currents flowing below the warm layers. As Westinghouse Electric describes it, "In an OTEC plant, a liquid like ammonia, which has a low boiling point, will be boiled by the ocean's warm surface, creating a gas at a pressure great enough to drive a turbine generator. After passing through the turbine, the gas will be cooled and condensed by cold water from the ocean depths."

Along with OTEC, other new forms of energy could be developed by the end of the next century. As an example, space satellites may collect solar energy and transmit it to earth via microwave. But the solar collectors would have to be so large that costs at present are prohibitive. Green plants might be developed and grown on a large scale for processing into commercial fuels. Hydrogen could be another energy source, although methods for "splitting water" (which generate hydrogen) on a large scale have not yet been established.

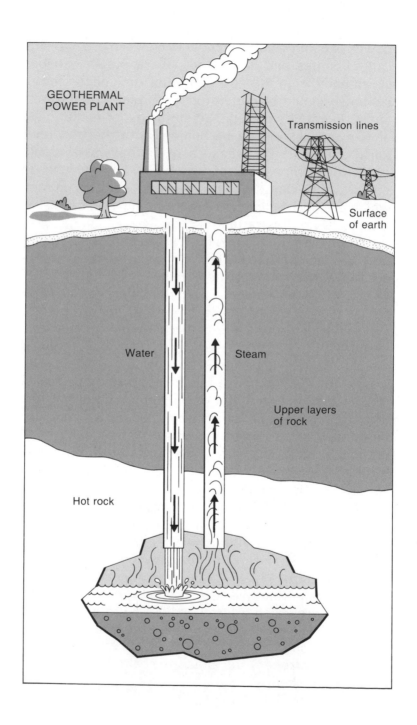

CONSERVATION

Along with developing renewable energy sources, an already affluent urban society can do more about conserving energy and limiting demands for fossil fuels. Ideally, this would mean encouraging people to use energy more efficiently—without waste—while continuing to maintain homes, businesses, industries, schools, hospitals, and many other needed facilities.

Major studies over the past decade (prepared for such institutions as the International Institute for Applied Systems Analysis in Austria and the National Science Foundation in the United States) indicate that carbon dioxide emissions will remain near today's level *if* industrialized nations use fuel more efficiently in cars and other forms of transportation; increase efforts to insulate buildings to conserve energy (whether used for heating or cooling); cut waste of energy in manufacturing and refrigeration; recycle garbage for fuel; and follow similar practices in other energy-consuming activities.

But there is another side to the coin. In less-developed countries, energy conservation often seems impractical and unfair. The "rich" nations of the world, such as the United States, Canada, Russia, and many European countries, account for three-fourths of the world fossil-fuel consumption and are responsible for most of the carbon dioxide buildup in the atmosphere. Third World nations are attempting to "catch up"—improving agricultural production, building industries, and urbanizing in general. The developing nations demand and consume more and more energy, most of it generated by fossil fuels.

In the past, the more industrialized and affluent nations have become, the more energy consumption has increased. Still, if Third World living standards improve—with better health, fewer infant deaths, improved income, and better quality of life—demographic experts (those who study population) see a leveling off of energy consumption. Birthrates in developing nations are expected to decrease. More children would survive early childhood, and Third World families would no longer have so many children to protect against losses due to high mortality rates among the very young.

In addition, energy analysts believe that conservation techniques, which help people produce and use energy more efficiently, will be cost effective and more widespread in the future. Thus more efficient energy use will prevent a drastic increase in consumption of nonrenewable fossil fuels.

There is also hope that the technology for developing renewable energy will be introduced on a global scale in the near future. However, this would require recognition by many governments that there is a connection between energy sources and carbon dioxide buildup. At present, some international research is being conducted on the causes and effects of climatic change. But scientists in many different disciplines say that energy and environmental policies must also be established to protect the interests of all nations.

What should such policies include? That is the big question. Nations usually weigh their own needs and concerns against the effects of global warming. Then governments attempt to determine what actions would best alleviate the buildup of greenhouse gases—a process that can be as complex as the climate system itself.

CHAPTER NINE

POLICY PROPOSALS AND PROBLEMS

Along with energy conservation and development of nonfossil energy sources, measures for dealing with the greenhouse threat have included proposals for banning the use of fossil fuels by placing high taxes on coal and conventional and synthetic oil and gas. Nonfossil fuels would be tax-free. Such a tax scheme could lower the worldwide energy demand, the EPA believes, and could shift consumption away from fuels high in carbon dioxide, although the demand for liquid fuels for transportation would remain high.

EFFECTS OF A
FOSSIL-FUEL BAN

Perhaps a worldwide tax on fossil fuels could greatly reduce carbon dioxide emissions, but little change is expected until the end of the next century. And global temperatures would continue to rise, although at a somewhat slower rate.

In addition, any major shift away from a major fuel source such as coal would lower the value of that resource and the income derived from industries that produce and transport the fuel and convert it into electricity. Such losses would have a significant effect on the United States, the Soviet Union, and China since these three nations have more than 80 percent of the world's known coal reserves.

M.I.T. scientists David Rose and Marvin Miller, with Carson Agnew of Stanford, pointed out in a recent issue of *Technology Review* that two of the nations with the most coal reserves (the United States and the USSR) could be "net losers as a result of global warming. Thus, in principle at least, these countries could mine enough coal to satisfy their own needs while curtailing exports in the name of 'responsible action' to deal with the CO_2 problem." But few believe such a policy would work, since large deposits of coal do exist in other parts of the world, such as India and Indonesia. Realistically, the "have-not" nations could not be expected to accept a ban on coal production while the "have" nations continued to exploit their supplies.

CONTROLLING CARBON DIOXIDE EMISSIONS

It is called the "technofix"—removing carbon dioxide from the atmosphere or from the smokestacks of coal-fired power plants via technical means. How would a technofix be accomplished? One proposal involves using powerful fans to draw in vast amounts of air that would then be treated to extract the carbon dioxide. But, as Dr. Gribbin writes in his study of carbon dioxide and the climate, "The power to drive these fans has to come from somewhere; and if the source was electricity from a fossil fuel power station, as much carbon dioxide would be released from fuel burnt to supply that energy as would be extracted from the air by the processing plant."

Carbon dioxide can be removed from flue gases emitted at power stations. But very expensive (estimated from 50 million to several hundred million dollars) pollution control devices called "scrubbers" would have to be installed, such as those suggested for removing sulfur dioxide—one of the forerunners of acid rain—from smokestacks. Another expensive technofix would be capturing and converting carbon dioxide in smokestacks to a gaseous liquid or solid form and then depositing it deep in the oceans.

Since power stations are responsible for less than 30 percent of the carbon dioxide emissions worldwide, most researchers believe that the costs for removal of carbon dioxide at coal-fired plants would be too high. The added expense could double, triple, or even quadruple electricity rates, depending on the efficiency of the carbon dioxide removal technology. Studies show that the costs of removing carbon dioxide at industrial sources could be much higher, so a technofix seems unlikely for the present.

FORESTATION AS A POLICY

Carbon dioxide can be stored in trees and other green plants, as described in earlier chapters. Some researchers have proposed that vast forestation projects could be undertaken in many different countries. Widespread tree planting would also help with such problems as erosion and loss of nutrients in the soil.

According to one study, sycamore seedlings would be the best trees for forestation, since they thrive in warm areas with little rainfall. But 2.5 million square miles (6.7 million sq. km)—land equal to the area of Europe—would be needed to plant enough sycamores for any effective removal of the 5 billion GT of carbon dioxide emitted each year. *If* that amount of land were planted, about 750 tons of carbon would be absorbed each growing year, and after some 50 years (when the sycamores had matured) an estimated 37,500 tons of carbon would be stored in each square kilometer of trees.

In theory, tree planting seems an attractive option for removing carbon dioxide from the atmosphere. Many countries could share in the effort without a heavy burden. But the drawbacks are almost insurmountable. A large portion—38 percent—of the total land on earth is already tree-covered, and another 9.5 percent is used for agriculture. Much of the remaining land is not suitable for planting. Besides, huge reforestation projects would require millions of tons of fertilizers. Although sufficient sources of nitrogen, phosphorus, and potash would probably be available, known reserves might be depleted or become scarce if fertilizers were used for vast tree plantings as well as for current consumption needs.

Costs, too, would be substantial, if not prohibitive. One study of a proposed reforestation project on .64 million square miles (1.77 million sq. km) of land in Hawaii put the total cost for land and irrigation systems at $400 billion. Additional large sums would be needed for fertilizers, pesticides, nurseries to grow seedlings, and other facilities and supplies.

There are other considerations as well. If huge tree plantations are going to be used as holding places for carbon, the earth's climate could be affected. For example, if trees are planted on what is now fallow land, the earth's albedo (reflective characteristic) could be altered. More of the sun's energy would be absorbed by the earth, which would increase the earth's temperature. Thus tree planting on a vast scale does not appear to be a practical option for controlling carbon dioxide, unless biological developments help produce trees capable of holding/storing much higher amounts of carbon.

OTHER OPTIONS

If huge tree-planting projects are not feasible for the present, at least reducing the rate of deforestation would be possible. Nations could also adopt policies to preserve land areas rich in carbon—grasslands and areas with extensive biota.

Another option for some countries is attempting to modify the weather and/or climate with such projects as cloud seeding to increase precipitation and injecting gases or chemicals into the stratosphere to reduce incoming solar radiation, thus decreasing the greenhouse effect—or so the theory suggests. However, researchers caution that other adverse effects on the environment could occur because of added chemicals.

Adapting to climatic change is one of the most probable alternatives for nations planning strategies to deal with carbon dioxide buildup in the atmosphere. Some of the agricultural and water resource adaptations were described in chapters 5 and 6. In addition, scientists are suggesting large-scale projects to remove salt from sea water and to obtain fresh water from icebergs, so that water could be supplied to regions that become arid. Other projects as part of national policy might include the development of crops that would grow in saline soil and ways to store and transport large amounts of water.

Not only would a nation have to maintain diverse sources of food and water (so that climatic changes would not destroy or greatly reduce expected supplies); a national policy would also have to encourage the development of nonfossil fuels and discourage those industries and activities that produce the most carbon dioxide emissions. If nations are to adapt successfully to global warming, they must also have strong economies, since changes cost money. In short, any adaptive policy amounts to finding many ways to build resilience—in agriculture, manufacturing, economics, politics, and so on—to cope with alterations in climate.

CHAPTER TEN

FROM GLOBAL PLANS TO CITIZEN ACTIONS

With all the possible policies that could be adopted to deal with the greenhouse effect, what programs are underway now? In the United States, the Department of Energy (DOE) has long supported major research on the relationship between energy-production activities and the effects of those activities on the atmosphere, including the greenhouse effect. The Department of Agriculture, the EPA, and NASA conduct related programs. Others include NSF-supported field, laboratory, and computer-modeling research of the atmosphere, part of which involves studies of trace gases and aerosols in both clean and polluted air.

WORLD WEATHER WATCHERS

The NSF also sponsors the Sea-Air Exchange (SEAREX) program. An international effort, SEAREX involves researchers in the United States, England, France, Australia, New Zealand, Japan, and China; the investigators are studying and measuring the atmospheric transport of trace elements and organic compounds from continental regions to the oceans.

The National Oceanic and Atmospheric Administration (NOAA) operates climate observatories in Alaska, Hawaii, American Samoa, and Antarctica. At remote clean-air sites, NOAA officials measure trace gases and particles in the atmosphere to determine concentrations that may have an impact on climate.

For more than a decade international organizations such as the World Meteorological Society, the United Nations Environmental Program, and the International Institute of Applied Systems Analysis have been studying atmospheric problems, including acid rain, the depletion of ozone, and carbon dioxide buildup.

In spite of all the research, there is little international agreement on what to do about environmental issues related to the atmosphere. As the EPA reports, "Countries are able to point to lingering uncertainties in the scientific evidence as the basis for inaction or delay." Economics is a barrier to international consensus as well, since some countries would have to pay more than others to reduce air pollution and the concentrations of carbon dioxide in the atmosphere. As mentioned in Chapter 8, industrialized nations depend on fossil fuels and have most of the resources, so they would have the most to lose by limiting fossil-fuel consumption. At the same time, developing countries need inexpensive fossil fuels to improve their living standards.

"Given these competing interests, the future of any international accord remains, at best, a distant prospect," the EPA concludes, adding, however, that "only an international response will be effective" in dealing with the greenhouse effect and other alterations in the atmosphere.

Climatologists worldwide agree and have called for a global scientific plan of action on tropospheric chemistry. It is in the troposphere, the layer of air closest to the earth's surface, that most weather and rapid temperature changes occur. The other three layers of air are the stratosphere, where ozone concentrates; the ionosphere, in which radio waves can travel long distances; and the exosphere, which is the layer of air just before interplanetary space.

All of the atmosphere is important to the life-support systems on earth, but the chemical makeup and cycles of the troposphere most directly affect people and other living organisms on the planet. In fact, the troposphere and biosphere are interdependent and constantly interact. An understanding of their interactions will help scientists determine more of the reasons for climatic change and what impact people have in altering climate.

A GLOBAL PROGRAM

In 1982 the Research Council of the NSF brought together fourteen scientists who formed a panel on global tropospheric chemistry. Supported by both the NSF and NASA, over the next year and a half, the panel developed a comprehensive plan for a Global Tropospheric Chemistry Program, which was published in 1984. A scientific strategy for action, the program has the following long-term goals: to understand the basic chemical cycles in the troposphere; to predict how those cycles would respond to disturbances brought on by natural and human activities; and to provide information needed to manage the chemistry of the atmosphere so that reactions are not adverse to global life-support systems.

In a summary of the program, the panel pointed out that highly skilled individuals and instrumentation are available for the research needed to attain the program goals, and they emphasized the importance of

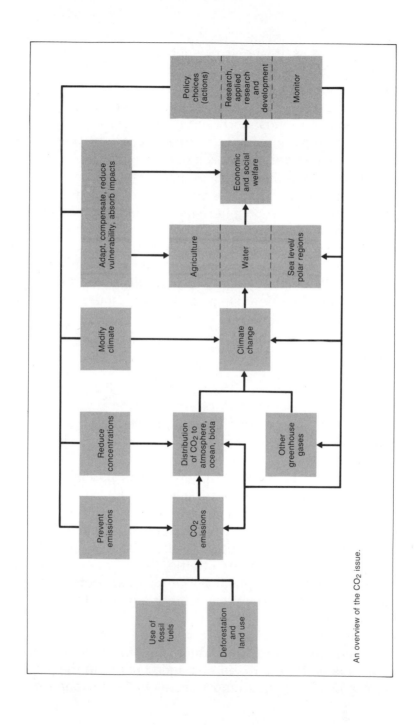

An overview of the CO_2 issue.

an international effort. However, the group recommended that the United States play a major role in pulling together scientists from a number of countries for cooperative studies in atmospheric chemistry. Cooperative research is essential, the panel believes, because the chemical systems under study are so complex and diverse, and "myriad sampling, analytical, and modeling tools" are needed. As the panel notes, global tropospheric chemistry research "will require the joint efforts of a broad spectrum of scientists: atmospheric chemists and physicists, marine chemists, meteorologists, ecologists, plant and soil biochemists, microbiologists, plant physiologists, laboratory chemists, geochemists, engineers, and others. An effort of this magnitude requires the cooperation and participation of universities, industry, and government agencies, both in the United States and in other countries."

HOW CITIZENS RESPOND

No doubt global scientific research will continue on the many possible effects of natural and human-induced chemical reactions in the atmosphere. But in the meantime, how should citizens with little understanding of atmospheric chemistry respond to an issue like the greenhouse threat?

Some may shrug off the problem as one too big or complex to solve, expressing a sense of futility with, "Nobody can control the weather anyway, so why worry about it?" Yet knowing about possible climatic alterations can help individuals make appropriate decisions to deal with such changes. In addition, some actions that could help reduce carbon dioxide accumulations in the atmosphere can also be beneficial in other ways.

One example is energy conservation. Since the early 1970s many people in industrialized nations have become more aware of threats to the environment and depletion of our nonrenewable resources. Along with such awareness have come energy shortages and cost boosts due to an oil embargo by the Organization of Petroleum Exporting Countries (OPEC), which controls prices and production of oil in the Middle East. Since the United States and other industrial nations are dependent on oil imports from OPEC, the embargo underscored the need to develop independent energy sources as well as use energy more efficiently.

As a result a variety of U.S. products, such as household appliances, have been designed and manufactured to use less energy. Automobiles are using less gasoline per mile, as mandated by the 1975 Energy Policy and Conservation Act. A number of major industrial firms have taken the necessary steps to reduce energy consumption in their manufacturing processes. Thousands of homes and other buildings have been insulated to save energy. And countless individuals and both public and private groups have found ways to save energy with conservation measures that range from recycling scrap metals and paper to developing systems for reusing water.

With all of these efforts, the amount of energy consumed for each dollar of the U.S. Gross National Product, or GNP (a ratio commonly used to measure energy demands), dropped dramatically from 1972 to 1982. According to the recent study by Rose, Miller, and Agnew published in *Technology Review*, the ratio of energy used per dollar of GNP decreased more than two percent per year, "driven by large increases in energy prices and a growing awareness that investments in more efficient use of energy pay well in terms of both economics and energy security. Many other OECD [Organization for Economic Cooperation and Development] countries did as well as the United States, or better. . . . Moreover, there is persuasive evidence that we are far from the limits of what can be achieved by more efficient energy usage." The study concludes that energy use could be cut in half by the year 2050, thus reducing carbon dioxide emissions by 50 percent.

Another example of citizen response to the carbon dioxide question and other atmospheric problems has been an increased effort to become more informed about how human activities affect the environment and the interrelationships of the various life systems on our planet. This is an essential aspect of any international action(s) to protect the environment.

Populations have to be well educated to understand and be willing to support life-preserving programs and policies. Learning about global warming from carbon dioxide concentrations in the atmosphere seems to be just one step forward in solving very complex environmental problems, not one of which is an isolated issue. Yet, as the Carbon Dioxide Assessment Committee has recommended in its various reports on the greenhouse effect, "research, monitoring, vigilance, and an open mind" are needed to develop any action program that will effectively deal with the carbon dioxide question—or, for that matter, other questions concerning our life-support systems on earth.

FOR FURTHER READING

Bernard, Harold W., Jr. *The Greenhouse Effect.* Cambridge, Mass.: Ballinger, 1980.

Global Tropospheric Chemistry Panel. *Global Tropospheric Chemistry.* Washington, D.C.: National Academy Press, 1984.

Gribbin, John. *Future Weather and the Greenhouse Effect.* New York: Delta/Eleanor Friede, 1982.

Halacy, D. S., Jr. *Ice or Fire? Surviving Climate Change.* New York: Harper & Row, 1978.

Hoffman, John S., Dale Keyes, and James G. Titus. *Projecting Future Sea Level Rise.* Washington, D.C.: U.S. Environmental Protection Agency, 1983.

Imbrie, John, and Katherine Palmer Imbrie. *Ice Ages: Solving the Mystery.* Hillside, N.J.: Enslow, 1979.

"Interview Roger Revelle." *Omni* Magazine. pp. 77 ff.

Nierenberg, William A., et al. *Changing Climate: Report of the Carbon Dioxide Assessment Committee.* Washington, D.C.: National Academy Press, 1983.

"Plowboy Interview Dr. Walter Orr Roberts: Living with the Greenhouse Effect." *Mother Earth News*, (March–April 1984): 17–22.

Rose, David J., Marvin M. Miller, and Carson Agnew. "Reducing the problem of Global Warming." *Technology Review*, (May/June 1984): 49–58.

Schell, Jonathan. *The Fate of the Earth.* New York: Alfred A. Knopf, 1982.

Schneider, Stephen H., and Randi Londer. *The Coevolution of Climate and Life.* San Francisco, Calif.: Sierra Club Books, 1984.

Seidel, Stephen, and Dale Keyes. *Can We Delay A Greenhouse Warming?* Washington, D.C.: U.S. Environmental Protection Agency, 1983.

Sheaffer, John R., and Leonard A. Stevens. *Future Water.* New York: William Morrow, 1983.

Smith, David G., Ed. *The Cambridge Encyclopedia of Earth Sciences.* New York: Crown/Cambridge University Press, 1981.

Wallace, Daniel, ed. *Energy We Can Live With.* Emmaus, Pa.: Rodale, 1976.

Woodwell, George M. "The Carbon Dioxide Question", *Scientific American*, (January 1978): 34–43.

INDEX

ABOUT THE AUTHOR

Kathlyn Gay has written books, magazine features, stories, and plays for both young readers and adults. Her book *Acid Rain*, published by Franklin Watts, was cited by both the National Council for the Social Studies and the National Science Teachers Association as one of the notable children's books for 1983.

Ms. Gay and her husband, Arthur L. Gay, live in Elkhart, Indiana.